BAROQUE TO MODERN

nentary Level

33 Pieces by 10 Composers in Progressive Order

Compiled and Edited by Richard Walters

On the cover:
Detail from *The Market Place and the Grote Kerk at Haarlem* (1674)
by Gerrit Berkheyde (1638–1698)

Detail from *Königstein mit roter Kirche* (1916)
Ernst Ludwig Kirchner (1880–1938)

ISBN 978-1-4950-8859-9

G. SCHIRMER, *Inc.*

DISTRIBUTED BY

7777 W. BLUEMOUND RD. P.O. BOX 13819 MILWAUKEE, WI 53213

www.musicsalesclassical.com
www.halleonard.com

CONTENTS

Though the table of contents appears in alphabetical order by composer, the music in this book is in progressive order.

COMPOSER BIOGRAPHIES, HISTORICAL NOTES AND PRACTICE AND PERFORMANCE TIPS

BÉLA BARTÓK

(1881–1945, Hungarian;
became a US citizen in 1945)

Béla Bartók is one of the most important and often performed composers of the twentieth century, and much of his music, including *Concerto for Orchestra*, his concertos, his string quartets, and his opera *Bluebeard's Castle*, holds a venerable position in the classical repertoire. His parents were amateur musicians who nurtured their young son with exposure to dance music, drumming, and piano lessons. In 1899 he started piano and composition studies at the Academy of Music in Budapest and not long after graduation he joined the Academy's piano faculty. Bartók wished to create music that was truly Hungarian at its core, a desire that sparked his deep interest in folk music. His work collecting and studying folksongs from around the Baltic region impacted his own compositional style greatly in terms of rhythm, mood, and texture. Bartók utilized folk influences to create a truly unique style. Though he composed opera, concertos, ballets, and chamber music, he was also committed to music education and composed several piano works for students, including his method *Mikrokosmos*. Bartók toured extensively in the 1920s and '30s, and became as well-known as both a pianist and composer. He immigrated to the US in 1940 to escape war and political turmoil in Europe, and settled in New York City, though the last years of his life were difficult, with many health problems.

Selections from *The First Term at the Piano*

(composed 1913)
With the original Hungarian title *Kezdõk zongoramuzsikája*, these 18 short pieces were selected from the 44 pieces Bartók composed for a piano method by Bartók and Sándor Reschofsky, published in 1913. The pieces were composed for piano students at Reschofsky's music school in Budapest. Some of the pieces are based on folksongs, others are original compositions. Fingerings, articulation and metronomic markings are by Bartók. After a series of setbacks and disappointments Bartók composed little in the years 1912–1914. His international acclaim and successful concert tours lay ahead, in the 1920s. The little pieces in *The First Term at the Piano* were the great composer's only compositions in 1913. In the previous year, 1912, Bartók prepared teaching editions of Bach, Beethoven, Haydn and Mozart which became standard pedagogical publications in Hungary.

Stepping Stones

Practice and Performance Tips

- As a companion exercise, practice a smooth five-finger pattern in both hands, from C to G and back down.
- This simple piece asks for an elegant phrase over three measures, played at ***f***.
- Smoothly move from note to note.
- There may be a slight *crescendo* and then *decrescendo* in each phrase.
- Use no pedal at all.

Follow the Leader

Practice and Performance Tips

- The piece is constructed in three four-measure phrases.
- The left hand leads in measures 1, 3 and 5, but in measures 2, 4 and 6–8 becomes accompaniment.
- Bartók's brief composition has vivid and essential details of accents, articulation and phrasing.
- Make certain to exactly execute all dynamics and articulations.
- The *sforzando* (***sf***) is to be played stronger than the accent (>).
- Keep the rhythm just as crisp in the middle soft section as in the surrounding loud sections.
- Measure 6 to the end requires independence of the hands in phrasing and articulation.
- Though Bartók's tempo is slow, your initial practice tempo can be even slower.
- Use no pedal at all.

Short and Long Legato

Practice and Performance Tips

- Each hand is in a five-finger position, A to E.
- The "short legato" of the title refers to the one-measure phrases, such as in the right hand measures 1–4.
- The "long legato" of the title refers to the long phrase in the left hand measures 1–4, or both hands measures 9–14.
- Notice how the few *staccato* notes create pleasing contrast in the musical texture.
- The entire piece needs a quiet, gentle touch.
- In measures 1–4 and 10–14 slightly bring out the melody in the right hand, with the left-hand accompaniment.
- Bartók's metronome indication is quite slow. Some may want to take the piece a bit faster.
- Create *legato* entirely with the fingers. Use no pedal at all.

Invention I

Practice and Performance Tips

- Though the composer has asked for ***f***, the piece needs *legato* and elegant phrasing.
- Practice hands separately in making a graceful phrase; then hands together, first slowly.
- Pay special attention to the composer's phrase markings.
- Your practice should lead to a steady, flowing line.
- Use no pedal at all.

CARL CZERNY
(1791–1857, Austrian)

Czerny began playing the piano at the age of three and was composing by the age of seven. His father was a piano teacher and supervised much of the boy's education until Czerny became one of Beethoven's students. From 1805 onward, Czerny dedicated much of his time to teaching, acquiring many famous students, including Liszt, Thalberg, and Leschetizky. Czerny often composed pieces for his students as an aid in developing a specific technical skill. In addition to his numerous pedagogical piano studies, for which he is best-remembered today, Czerny published hundreds of other works, including symphonies, variations, arrangements, chamber music, and sacred choral pieces.

Exercise in C Major
from The Little Pianist, Op. 823, No. 6

Practice and Performance Tips

- Both hands are in a five-finger position for the entire piece.
- The composer provided no tempo for this exercise. The bracketed information is an editorial suggestion.
- Notice Czerny's articulation. Play the notes in the three-note slurs smoothly. The repeated notes, such as in measures 2 and 4, should be played with slight separation.
- Even though the music is simple, Czerny challenges the beginning player by marking it ***p***, which requires some finesse and subtlety in the tone.

CORNELIUS GURLITT
(1820–1901, German)

Many of Gurlitt's piano works have colorful, descriptive names, which is no surprise given his lifelong interest in art. He studied music in Leipzig, Copenhagen, and Rome, where he was nominated an honorary member of the papal academy Di Santa Cecilia. His brother Louis was a very successful artistin Rome, and Cornelius himself studied painting for a time while living there. Gurlitt worked as a pianist and church organist, and also served as a military band master. He returned to his hometown of Altona, where the Duke of Augustenburg hired him as music teacher for three of his daughters. Gurlitt wrote symphonies, songs, operas, and cantatas, but he is best remembered today for his pedagogical keyboard pieces.

Lesson No. 1 from *The First Lessons,* Op. 117

Practice and Performance Tips

- Both hands are in a five-finger position throughout.
- Notice the two-measure phrases in measures 9–10, 11–12, 13–14, and measure 16 in the left hand only.
- The first eight measures have no phrasing, and each note is distinctly played.
- Gurlitt challenges the student by giving a dynamic of ***p***. Playing with good tone and evenness softly takes practice!

Lesson No. 2 from *The First Lessons,* Op. 117

Practice and Performance Tips

- As in Lesson No. 1, both hands are in a five-finger position throughout.
- There is rhythmic independence of the hands in measures 1–4 and 9–12.
- Notice the left-hand phrase in measures 2, 4, 10 and 12. Also, observe the quarter-note rest on beat 4 in these measures.
- Use the dynamic markings to make the piece interesting. Gurlitt marks ***f*** for measures 1–4, then scales back to ***mf*** with a *crescendo* back to ***f*** in measure 9.

Lesson No. 3 from *The First Lessons,* Op. 117

Practice and Performance Tips

- Long held notes in one hand are accompaniment to moving notes in the other hand in measures 1–16.
- Both hands play the same notes in octaves, at ***ff***, in the last eight measures.
- The right hand remains in a five-finger position throughout, C to G, but the second finger crosses the thumb in measures 12 and 16.
- After beginning with the second finger on C at the beginning, the left hand changes hand position in measure 9, with the fifth finger on C.
- Notice the quick change of dynamic, from ***p*** in measures 1–8 to ***f*** in measure 9.

Lesson No. 6 from *The First Lessons,* Op. 117

Practice and Performance Tips

- The piece is clearly in three sections: measures 1–8; measures 9–16; and measures 17–24.
- Observe the contrasts in dynamics in each of the three sections.
- All eighth notes are marked with a slur and are to be played smoothly.
- Make sure to observe the quarter-note rests in the left hand in measures 11 and 13–16 (also in measure 20).
- The rest in measure 9 allows the left hand to move up to a new hand position.

Lesson No. 9 from *The First Lessons,* Op. 117

Practice and Performance Tips

- To play this short waltz exactly as written is challenging enough, but moreover the composer asked for no dynamic changes throughout.
- The challenge is to correctly observe the rests on beat 3 after the half notes in both the right and left hands. The tendency is to hold the half note an extra beat.
- Precisely release the half notes on beat 3. This will give the music rhythmic crispness.
- Use no sustaining pedal.

GEORGE FRIDERIC HANDEL

(1685–1759, German/British)

Handel was one of the defining composers of the Baroque period. After a brief time in Italy as a young man, he spent nearly his entire adult career in London, where he became famous as a composer of opera and oratorio, including *Messiah*, now his most recognizable music. Handel also wrote numerous concertos, suites, overtures, cantatas, trio sonatas, and solo keyboard works. Though he taught some students early in his career and occasionally instructed members of the London aristocracy, Handel was not known for his teaching abilities. His keyboard works were likely not written for any of his students, but to fulfill commissions or generate income from publication. Handel composed various keyboard works until 1720, then he became master of the orchestra for the Royal Academy of Music, an organization dedicated to performing new operas. After Italian opera fell out of fashion in London, Handel turned his compositional efforts to oratorio.

Passepied in C Major, HWV 559

Practice and Performance Tips

- A passepied (pronounced pass-uh-pee-ay) is a lively French dance in triple meter from the Baroque era.

- Except those marked with a slur (measures 7–10), all quarter notes should be played slightly detached.
- Observing the comment above, as well as the suggested slurs and sudden changes in dynamics will create the right Baroque style.
- Use no sustaining pedal.

DMITRI KABALEVSKY

(1904–1987, Russian)

Kabalevsky was an important Russian composer of the Soviet era who wrote music in many genres, including four symphonies, a handful of operas, theatre and film scores, patriotic music, choral music, vocal music, and numerous piano works. He embraced the Soviet notion of socialist realism in art, a fact that was politically advantageous to his career in the USSR. While studying piano and composition at the Moscow Conservatory, he taught piano lessons at a music college and it was for these students that he began writing works for young players. In 1932 he started teaching at the Moscow Conservatory, earning the title of professor in 1939. He eventually went on to develop programs for the concert hall, radio, and television aimed at teaching children about classical music. In the last decades of his life, Kabalevsky focused on developing music curricula for schools, retiring from the Moscow Conservatory to teach in public schools where he could test his theories and the effectiveness of his syllabi. This he considered his true life's work, and his pedagogical principles revolutionized music education in Russia. A collection of his writings on music education was published in English in 1988 as *Music and Education: A Composer Writes About Musical Education*.

Selections from *24 Pieces for Children,* Op. 39

(composed 1944)

Kabalevsky began writing piano music for students as early as 1927. His first major set, *30 Children's Pieces*, Op. 27, was composed in 1937–38. The *24 Pieces for Children* (alternately titled *24 Easy Pieces*), Op. 39 is for an earlier level of study than Op. 27. Though Kabalevsky composed operas, orchestral music, concertos and chamber music throughout his career, as well as more difficult piano literature, he returned to writing music for piano students periodically in his life, reflecting his deeply felt commitment to music education.

Melody (No. 1)

Practice and Performance Tips

- Make a graceful phrase in both hands.
- Practice hands separately in making the phrase.
- If small hands cannot achieve a *legato* sound using the fingers only in the left hand, very sparing use of the sustaining pedal can be used to create the smooth movement from chord to chord.
- Note the dynamic contrasts, with a sudden ***p*** in measure 5, followed by a *crescendo.*

Polka (No. 2)

Practice and Performance Tips

- For the first time in the progressive order of the book the melody moves to the left hand.
- The right hand plays an accompaniment.
- Practice hands separately.
- Note the smooth phrasing in the left hand and the staccato markings in the right hand.
- Then slowly practice hands together, exactly retaining the articulation Kabalevsky has composed.
- The challenge is to combine playing the left hand smoothly and the right hand staccato.

Rambling (No. 3)

Practice and Performance Tips

- Note the combination of *staccato* and sustained notes (with *tenuto* markings) in the right hand.
- Practice right hand only, carefully playing the composed articulations.
- Play the *staccato/tenuto* combination in the left hand as if it were an eighth note followed by an eighth rest.
- Practice hands together slowly, executing all the articulation exactly as composed.
- Use no pedal at all.

Cradle Song (No. 4)

Practice and Performance Tips

- Both hands play the same notes, in octaves, throughout. First practice hands separately.
- Practice may begin at ***mf***.
- After becoming secure in the piece, then play softly and gently, but steadily.
- Create the two-note slur with *legato*, with a very slight lift before the next two-note slur.
- Note the composer's tempo marking of *poco lento.*
- Think of the tempo as gently rocking a baby's cradle back and forth.
- Use no pedal at all.
- Possible slight *rit.* in the final measure leading to the final note.

Funny Event (No. 7)

Practice and Performance Tips

- The entire piece is constructed of two-measure phrases, with one hand imitating the other.
- Every note is played *staccato*.
- Note the accents on the downbeats of measures 1–8 and measures 17–24.
- There are three sections to the form: measures 1–8, measures 9–16, and measures 17–24 (repeat of measures 1–8).
- Though still *staccato*, the dynamics and texture are markedly different in the middle section.
- Your practice tempo can begin as slowly as necessary to keep a steady beat.
- Gradually increase the tempo in your practice as you master the music, maintaining steadiness whatever the tempo.
- Your performance should be playful and witty, to reflect the title.
- Use no pedal at all.

Scherzo (No. 12)

Practice and Performance Tips

- This short piece can create a brilliant effect.
- Because it is so short when played at a fast tempo, one might repeat the entire piece.
- Practice should begin hands together at a slow tempo.
- From the beginning of practice, learn the articulation with the notes.
- Note the slurred three notes in the left hand, answered by two notes marked *staccato* in the right hand.
- The contrast between the slur and the *staccato* creates the essential character of the music.
- Use no pedal at all.

Selections from 35 *Easy Pieces,* Op. 89

(composed 1972–74)

Kabalevsky's last large set of piano pieces for students was composed in his late sixties, after a lifetime of experiences with young musicians, and after he had long since attained a revered position as the cultural leader of music education in the USSR. These were also his last compositions for piano. After 1974 Kabalevsky only wrote a few more compositions, which were songs or small choral pieces.

First Piece (No. 1)

Practice and Performance Tips

- Make a graceful phrase in the right hand, and answer it with a graceful phrase in the left hand.
- Smoothly pass the phrase from the right to the left hand in measures 9–10 and 11–12.
- Note the progression from ***p*** to ***mf*** and back to ***p*** in this brief piece.
- Gently and gracefully cross the left hand over for the final note.
- Use no pedal at all.

Quiet Song (No. 3)

Practice and Performance Tips

- The right hand changes position in measure 4, then again in measures 7, 11 and 14.
- The left hand changes position in measures 6 and 13.
- Take special note of the composer's phrase markings, and smoothly pass the phrase from the right to the left hand.
- Practice at mf until you are confident, then begin practicing at ***p***. Note the title of the piece!
- *Cantabile* means a singing tone, which implies smooth playing.
- Use no pedal at all.

At Recess (No. 4)

Practice and Performance Tips

- The piece is comprised of three elements: two-note slurs, *staccato* notes, and four-note phrases.
- Each element must be precisely played to create the playful spirit of "At Recess."
- Make certain to smoothly move from right hand to left hand in measures 8 and 15.
- Though played ***f***, this piece still requires a buoyant touch.
- Practice slowly with both hands together.
- Use no pedal at all.

Light and Shadow (No. 7)

Practice and Performance Tips

- The "light" is the loud music; the "shadow" is the soft music.
- Notice the contrast between the *staccato* markings and those notes without *staccato*.
- Be careful not to play all notes *staccato*.
- First practice hands separately, slowly.
- Then practice hands together, slowly.
- Retain the composed articulation in your practice, no matter what tempo.
- Use no pedal at all.

Little Hedgehog (No. 8)

Practice and Performance Tips

- Notice that every note of the piece is played *staccato*, with the final three notes also accented.

- Kabalevsky has indicated *staccatissimo*, meaning extremely short, crisp *staccato*.
- Practice right and left hands separately, and initially at a slow tempo.
- The sudden ***p*** in measure 8 followed by the *crescendo* creates a fun effect.
- Use no pedal at all.

Trumpet and Echo (No. 15)

Practice and Performance Tips

- The right hand is the trumpet and the left hand is the echo.
- The right hand plays ***f***, with each note articulated and accented.
- In contrast, the left hand plays softly and *legato*, moving from note to note smoothly.
- The composer's marking *marcato* refers to the right hand only.
- Practice hands together, first at a slow tempo.
- Use no pedal at all.

Trumpet and Drum (No. 20)

Practice and Performance Tips

- The left hand represents the drum throughout, which should be played *marcato* and very steadily.
- The right hand is the trumpet.
- Accurately play the two-note slurs in the right hand.
- Carefully and enthusiastically play the accents as the composers has indicated.
- Even though the piece begins ***f***, in measure 13 the composer asks for even more volume.
- Use no pedal at all.

LOUIS KÖHLER

(1820–1886, German)

His full name was Christian Louis Heinrich Köhler. After study in Vienna in piano, he settled in Königsberg, Germany, where he remained for the rest of his life. Köhler was a noted music critic for decades writing in the Königsberg newspaper, the *Königsberger Hartungsche Zeitung*, and for other publications. Among his compositions are three operas, a ballet, and many pieces for student pianists. Among these is *Die allerleichtesten Übungsstücke* (The Easiest Exercises).

Imitation from *The Easiest Exercises*, Op. 190, Nos. 13 and 14

Practice and Performance Tips

- As its title suggests, the second eight measures imitate the first, but move the melody to the left hand and the whole note accompaniment to the right hand.
- This was originally two short pieces. We combined them as one piece for this edition.
- Practice slowly and evenly until your left hand in measures 9–16 can match the tempo of the right hand in measures 1–8.

Melody in C Major from *The Easiest Exercises*, Op. 190, No. 16

Practice and Performance Tips

- The composer keeps the right hand simpler while the left hand has more movement.
- The right hand is in a five-finger position, C to G; but the left hand expands that by one note.
- In the left hand, the fifth finger alternates between C and the B below it.
- In this exercise the composer introduces the student to "Alberti bass," which outlines the notes of a chord. This must be played very steadily as a foundation accompaniment for the melody.

Traveling from *The Easiest Exercises*, Op. 190, No. 17

Practice and Performance Tips

- Köhler expands on the introduction of the "Alberti bass" in the left hand from exercise 16 in the one that follows it.
- As the student progresses, Köhler asks for more details in playing, such as adding articulations: accents, slurs, and *staccato* markings.
- Use the articulation to create a well-sculpted and interesting performance.
- Notice the *staccato* marking for the quarter note on beat 3 of measure 12.
- The left-hand accompaniment figure should be slightly softer than the right-hand melody.

JEAN-JOSEPH MOURET

(1682–1738, French)

Born in the southern French town Avignon, Mouret moved to Paris in his twenties, where he gained patronage from aristocrats. He primarily composed works that were in that period a combination of opera and ballet, but also various instrumental compositions. For twenty years he was music director of the Nouveau Théatre Italien, where he composed incidental music for comedies. He jealously competed with the far more successful

Jean-Philippe Rameau in the elite Parisian music scene. Though Mouret moved in fashionable circles and was a notable figure for a time, he died in poverty. His music is largely forgotten today, except for the Fanfare Rondeau, which became famous as the theme of the long-running television series *Masterpiece Theatre*. It is from his first *Suite de symphonie*, composed in 1729, for oboes, bassoon, trumpets, violins, double bass and timbales.

Fanfare Rondeau

Practice and Performance Tips

- The melody line in the right hand is for trumpet in the original music. Imagine a stately, majestic trumpet sound as you play.
- The left-hand bass line supports the melody.
- Practice slowly until you can maintain a very steady, strong beat. Then move gradually to a performance tempo.
- Whatever the tempo, keep it very steady throughout.
- The end of measure 16 begins the "B" middle section. In the original orchestration the violins took the melody here. Make a contrast by quickly shifting to ***p***.
- A crescendo leads into the return of the opening theme in measures 23–24.

DMITRI SHOSTAKOVICH

(1906–1975, Russian)

A major mid-20th century composer, Shostakovich is famous for his epic symphonies, concertos, operas, string quartets, and other chamber works. Born in St. Petersburg, his entire career took place in Soviet-era Russia. His life teetered between receiving high official honors and living with an almost debilitating fear of arrest for works that did not adhere to the Soviet ideals of socialist realism. In 1934, his opera *Lady Macbeth of the Mtsensk District* met with great popular success, but was banned by Stalin for the next thirty years as modernist, surrealist, and obscene. The following year, Stalin began a campaign known as the Purges, executing or exiling to prison camps politicians, intellectuals, and artists. Shostakovich managed to avoid such a fate, and despite an atmosphere of anxiety and repression, was able to compose an astounding number of works with originality, humor, and emotional power. He succeeded in striking a balance between modernism and tradition that continues to make his music accessible to a broad audience. An excellent pianist, Shostakovich performed concertos by Mozart, Prokofiev, and Tchaikovsky early in his career, but after 1930 limited himself to performing his own works and some chamber music. He taught instrumentation and composition at the Leningrad Conservatory from 1937–1968, with brief breaks due to war and other political disruptions, and at the Moscow Conservatory in the 1940s. Since his death in 1975, Shostakovich has become one of the most-performed 20th century composers.

Selections from *Children's Notebook for Piano,* Op. 69

(composed 1944–45)

Among a huge output of symphonies, operas and chamber music, Shostakovich wrote only a few pieces for piano students. *Children's Notebook for Piano* was written for his eight-year-old daughter, Galina, for her studies on the instrument. The original set was published as six pieces. The seventh piece, "Birthday," written for Galina's ninth birthday in 1945, was added in a later edition.

March (No. 1)

Practice and Performance Tips

- Pay attention to dynamic contrast from the *diminuendo* in measures 7–8 to the sudden ***f*** at measure 9, and then again from measures 11–12 to the ***f*** at 13.
- A march requires a particularly steady beat. Begin with a slow practice tempo.
- Use no pedal at all.

Waltz (No. 2)

Practice and Performance Tips

- The melody is in the right hand throughout; the left hand is accompaniment.
- Play the right-hand melody with slightly more volume than the left hand.
- In measure 20 the melody lands on a B-flat – the first black note in the piece and the entrance to a new key area. Try a color change here to make it more special.
- The piece could be very well played with no pedal throughout, or careful touches of pedal could be added.

DANIEL GOTTLOB TÜRK

(1750–1813, German)

Educated first by his musical father and then at the University of Leipzig, Türk studied with several of Bach's students and finally decided on a career in music. In 1774 he became the Kantor at the Ulrichskirche in Halle, and later the director of music at Halle University, as well as the music director at the Marktkirche. Beyond his teaching and church responsibilities he completed and published several books on the practicalities of being a church organist, improving church music, a textbook on keyboard playing, and various other theoretical and scientific works related to music. Though remembered today as a writer and advocate of music, he composed a notable output of works, of which several short keyboard pieces are still played.

The Scales
from *120 Pieces for the Aspiring Pianist,* No. 6

Practice and Performance Tips

- This music, featuring eighth notes moving in scale-like patterns, should be played with lightness and clarity.
- Grouping the eighth notes in four-note slurs, as suggested, will give the piece some style.
- Also, playing the first section ***p***, then suddenly switching to ***mf*** on the last note of measure 8 will give some liveliness.
- Make sure to keep a very steady beat and play evenly.
- No sustaining pedal.

Sad Feelings
from *120 Pieces for the Aspiring Pianist,* No. 14

Practice and Performance Tips

- Playing *legato* throughout will help create the sad mood of the music.
- Play at a slow and steady tempo, giving the piece full dignity.
- The soft dynamic is interrupted with accents on beat 1 in measures 6 and 7.
- A very slight slowing down might be added in the final measure only.
- No sustaining pedal.

WILHELM MORITZ VOGEL
(1846–1922, German)

Pianist and composer Vogel was born at Sorgau, then part of Silesia, and studied at the Conservatory at Leipzig. He remained in that city, working as a music critic, choral conductor, teaching piano, and writing music for students. Vogel left few known works. They include a set of piano pieces, *Kinderleben* (*Children's Life*), *Kleine Elementar-Musiklehre* (*Little Elementary Music Theory*), some art song duets, and this little march for piano, written for piano students.

March in C Major

Practice and Performance Tips

- A march always needs a sturdy, strong beat.
- A fun way to find a tempo of a march is to walk as a soldier or a band in a parade.
- The left hand remains in the same five-note hand position throughout.
- The quarter notes should not be played smoothly, but rather punched individually, to give the force of the march.
- In contrast, the eighth notes should be slurred, as marked.
- Use no sustaining pedal.

— Richard Walters, editor

LABORUM
DULCE
LENIMEN
G. SCHIRMER

These pieces were previously published in the following Schirmer Performance Editions volumes.

Bartók: Stepping Stones from *The First Term at the Piano*
Bartók: Follow the Leader from *The First Term at the Piano*
Bartók: Short and Long Legato from *The First Term at the Piano*
Bartók: Invention I from *The First Term at the Piano*
from *The 20th Century: Elementary Level*
edited by Richard Walters

Melody
Polka
Rambling
Cradle Song
Funny Event
Scherzo
from *Kabalevsky: 24 Pieces for Children, Op. 39*
edited by Margaret Otwell

First Piece
Quiet Song
At Recess
Light and Shadow
Little Hedgehog
Trumpet and Echo
Trumpet and Drum
from *Kabalevsky: 35 Easy Pieces, Op. 89*
edited by Richard Walters

March
Waltz
from *Shostakovich: Children's Notebook for Piano, Op. 69*
edited by Richard Walters

First Piece

from *35 Easy Pieces*

Dmitri Kabalevsky
Op. 89, No. 1

Andante [𝅗𝅥 = c. 66–72]

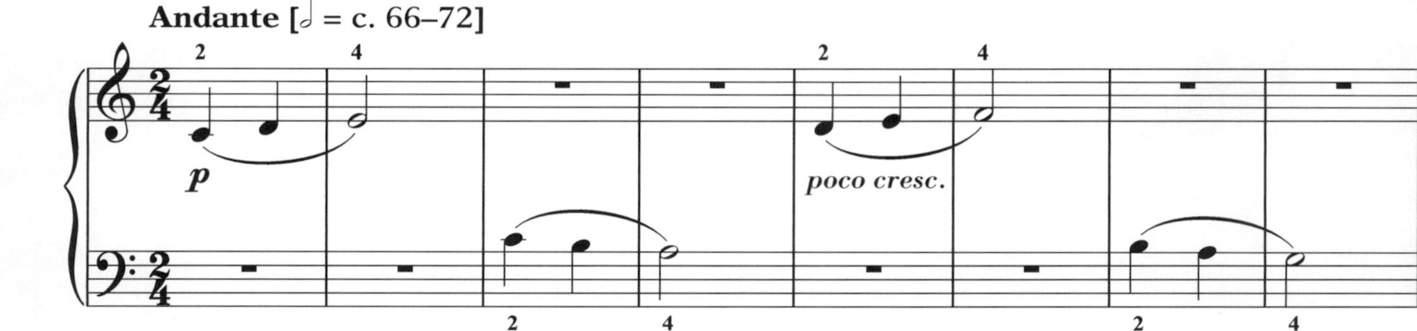

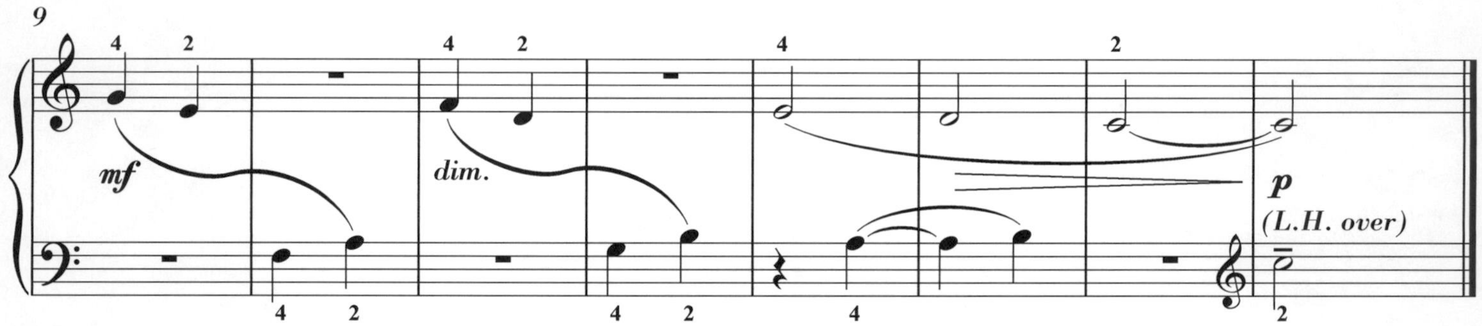

Fingerings are by the composer.

Stepping Stones

from *The First Term at the Piano*

Béla Bartók

Moderato ♩ = 96

Fingerings are by the composer.

Melody

from *24 Pieces for Children*

Dmitri Kabalevsky
Op. 39, No. 1

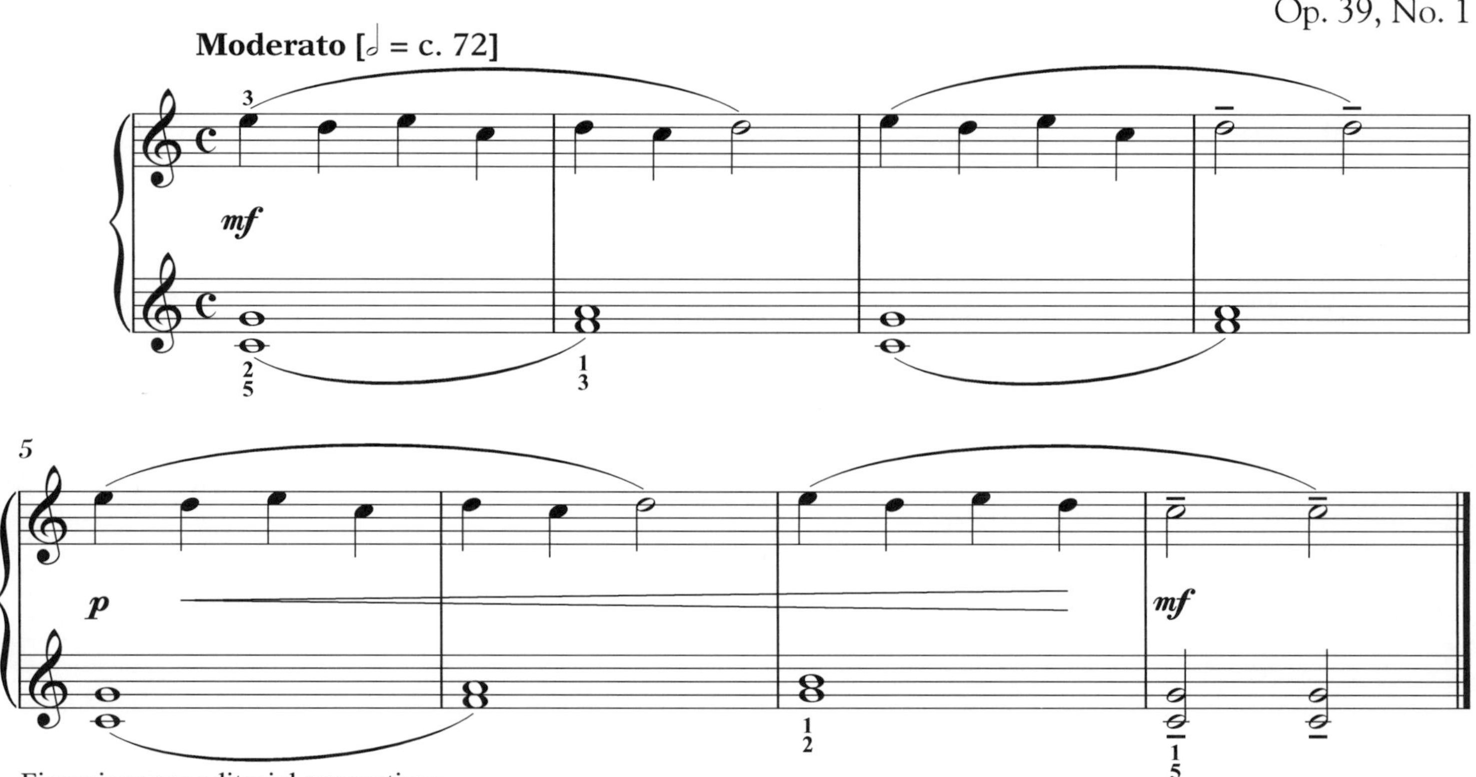

Fingerings are editorial suggestions.

Cradle Song

from *24 Pieces for Children*

Dmitri Kabalevsky
Op. 39, No. 4

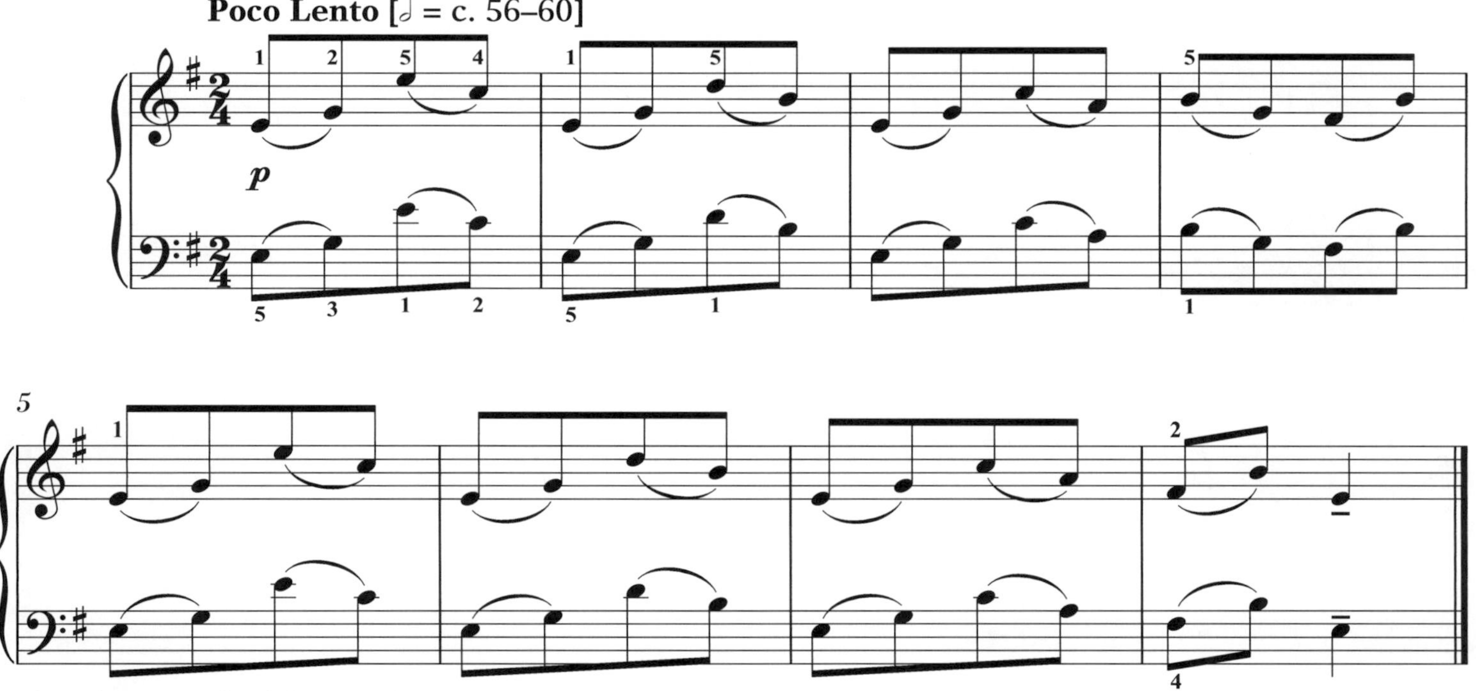

Fingerings are editorial suggestions.

Quiet Song

from *35 Easy Pieces*

Dmitri Kabalevsky
Op. 89, No. 3

Fingerings are by the composer.

Rambling

from *24 Pieces for Children*

Dmitri Kabalevsky
Op. 39, No. 3

Fingerings are editorial suggestions.

Lesson No. 1

from *The First Lessons*

Cornelius Gurlitt
Op. 117, No. 1

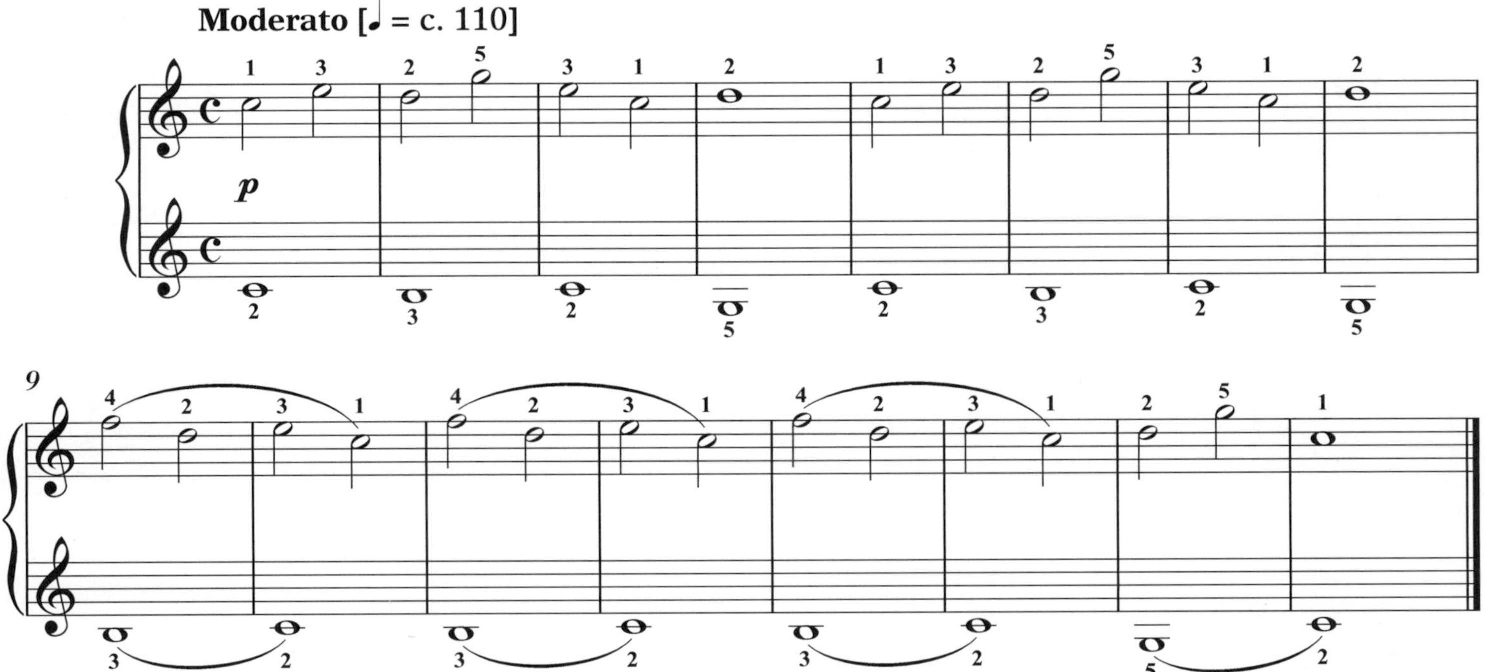

Fingerings are by the composer.

Lesson No. 2

from *The First Lessons*

Cornelius Gurlitt
Op. 117, No. 2

Fingerings are by the composer.

At Recess

from *35 Easy Pieces*

Dmitri Kabalevsky
Op. 89, No. 4

Allegro [♩ = c. 120]

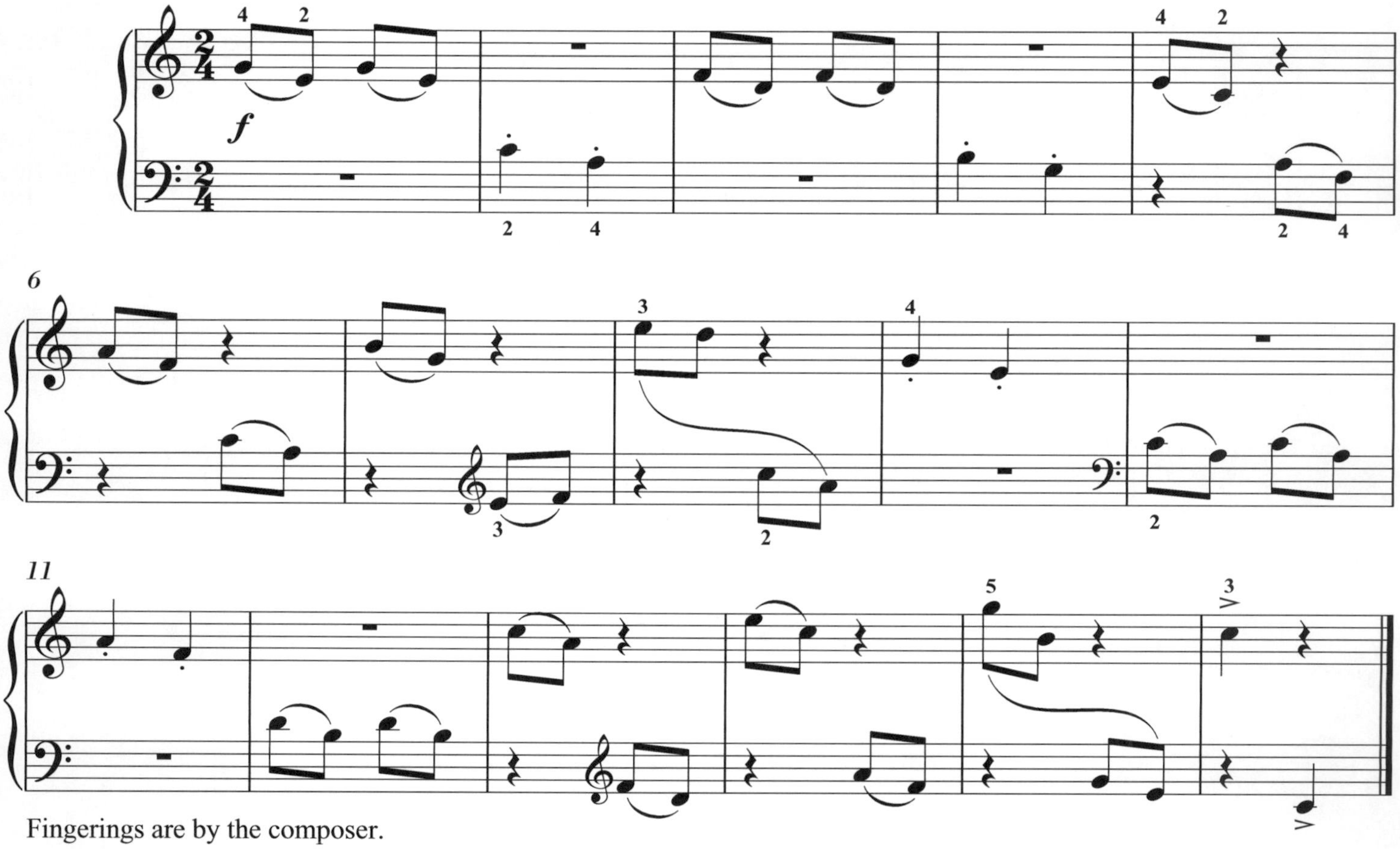

Fingerings are by the composer.

Trumpet and Echo

from *35 Easy Pieces*

Dmitri Kabalevsky
Op. 89, No. 15

Marcato [♩ = c. 112]

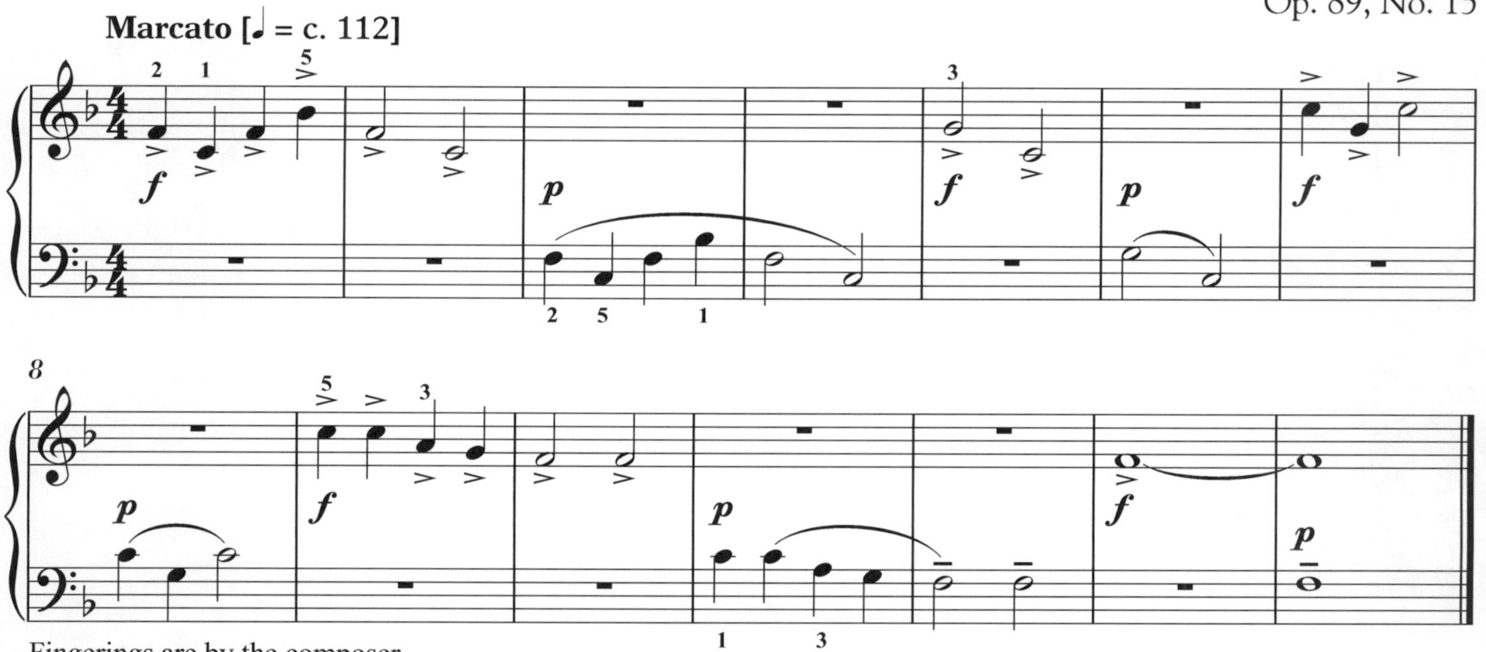

Fingerings are by the composer.

Little Hedgehog

from *35 Easy Pieces*

Dmitri Kabalevsky
Op. 89, No. 8

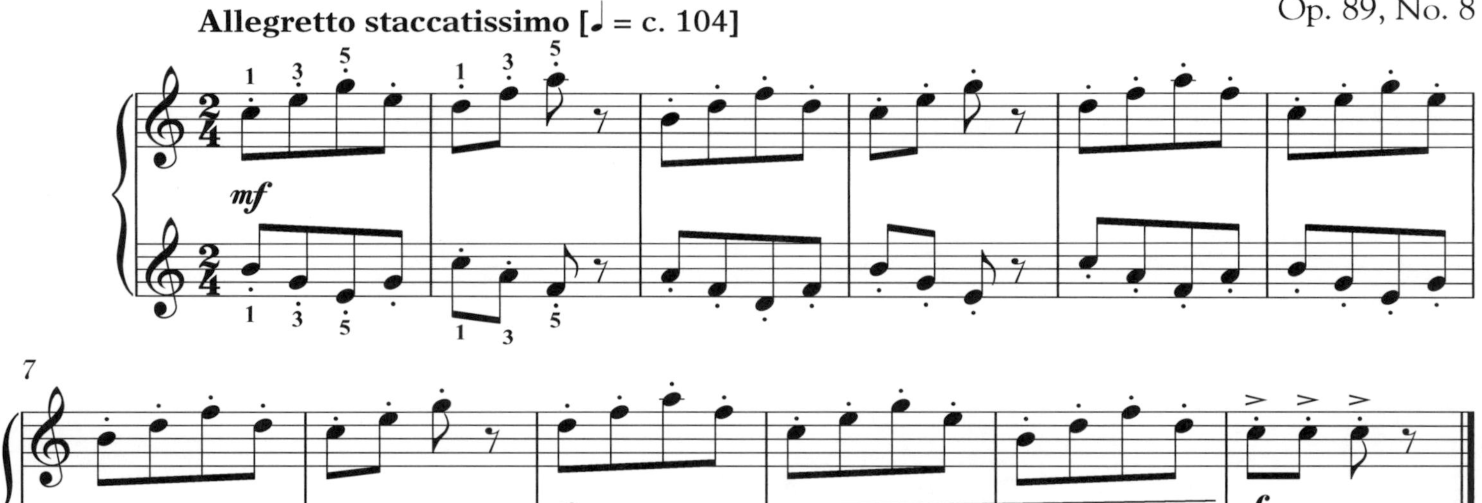

Allegretto staccatissimo [♩ = c. 104]

Fingerings are by the composer.

Light and Shadow

from *35 Easy Pieces*

Dmitri Kabalevsky
Op. 89, No. 7

Moderato [♩ = c. 104]

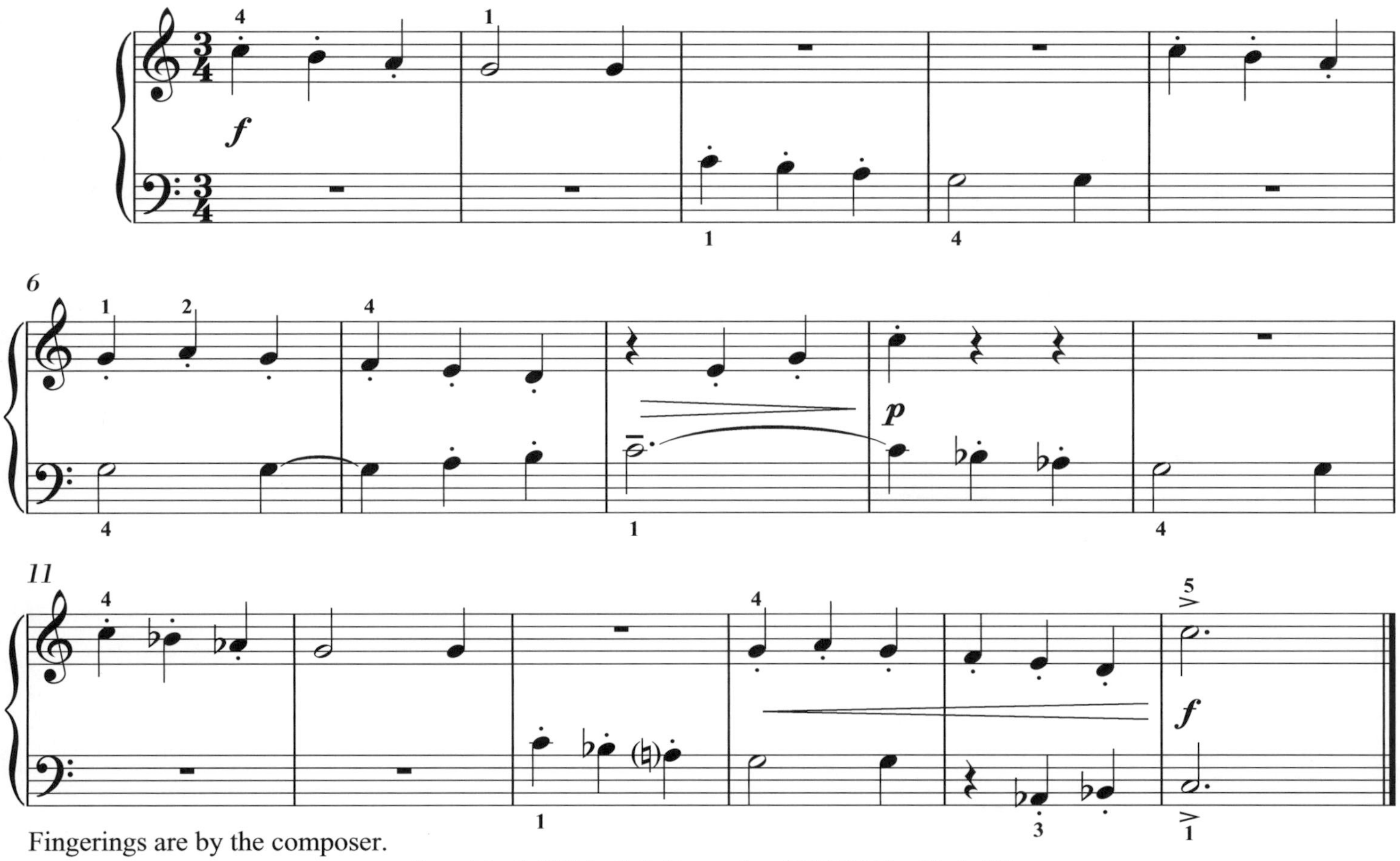

Fingerings are by the composer.

March in C Major

Wilhelm Moritz Vogel

Moderato [♩ = c. 132]

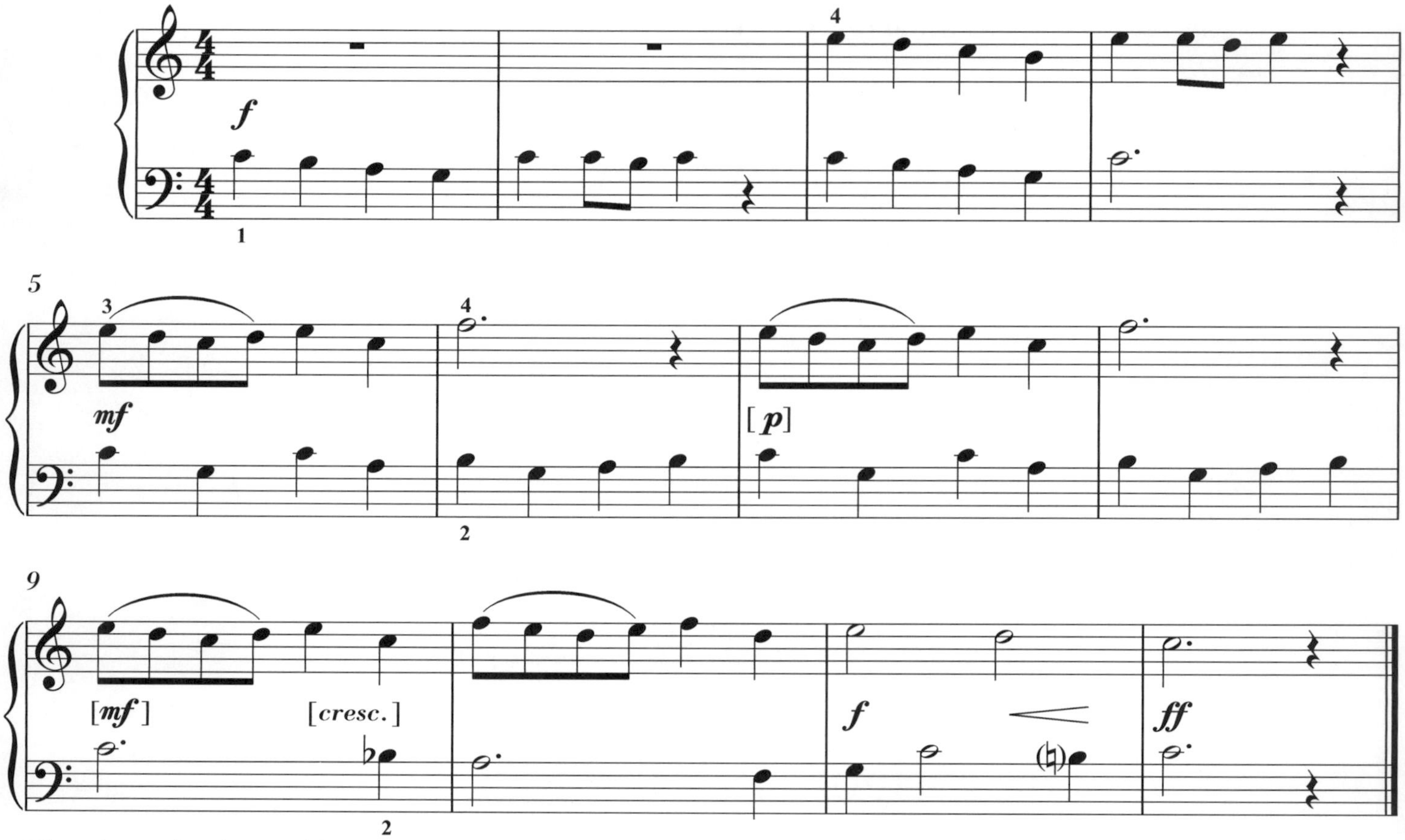

Fingerings, phrasing, and bracketed dynamics are editorial suggestions.

Polka

from *24 Pieces for Children*

Dmitri Kabalevsky
Op. 39, No. 2

Allegretto [♩ = c. 128]

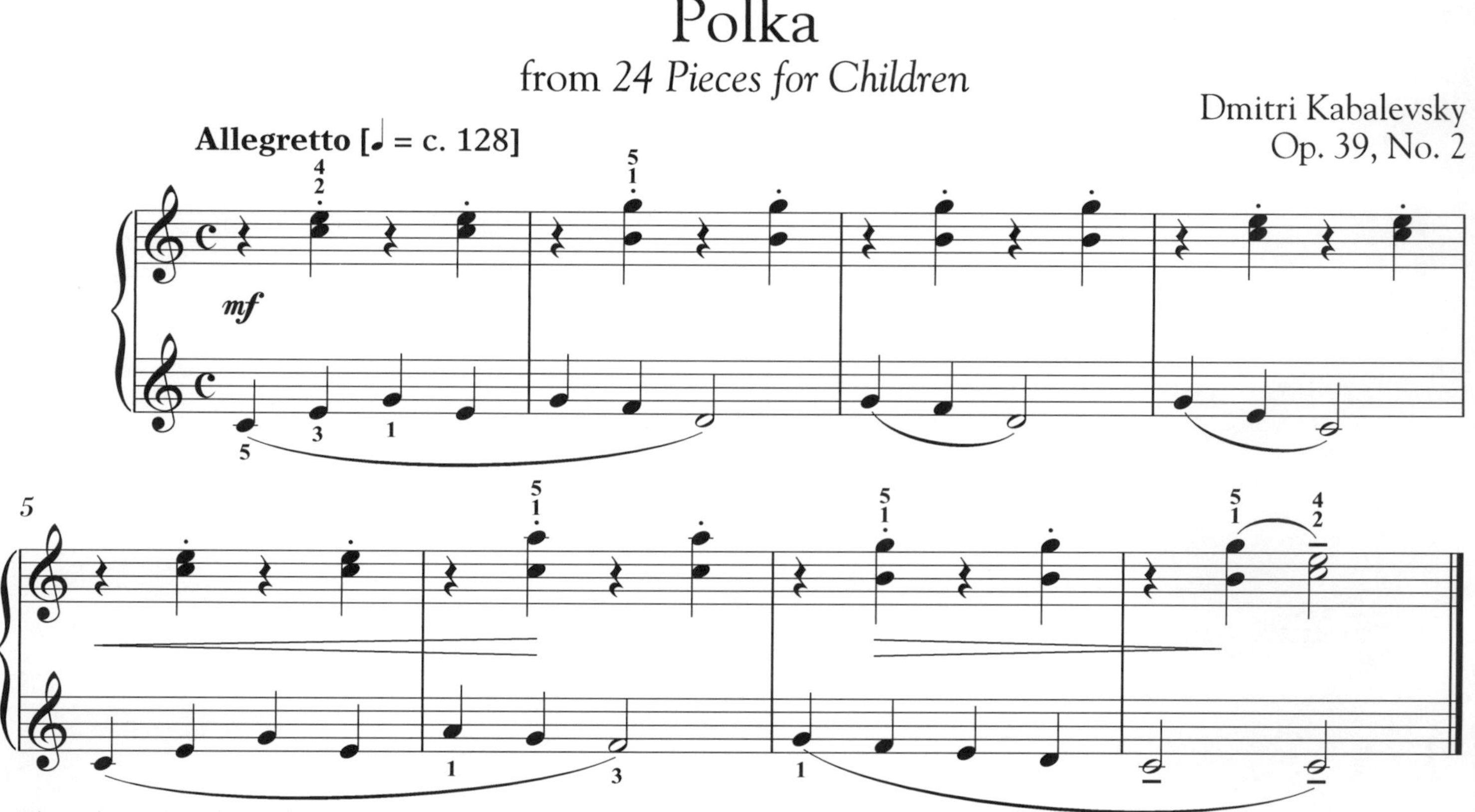

Fingerings are editorial suggestions.

Funny Event

from *24 Pieces for Children*

Dmitri Kabalevsky
Op. 39, No. 7

Fingerings are editorial suggestions.

Melody in C Major

from *The Easiest Exercises*

Louis Köhler
Op. 190, No. 16

Fingerings are by the composer.

Traveling

from *The Easiest Exercises*

Louis Köhler
Op. 190, No. 17

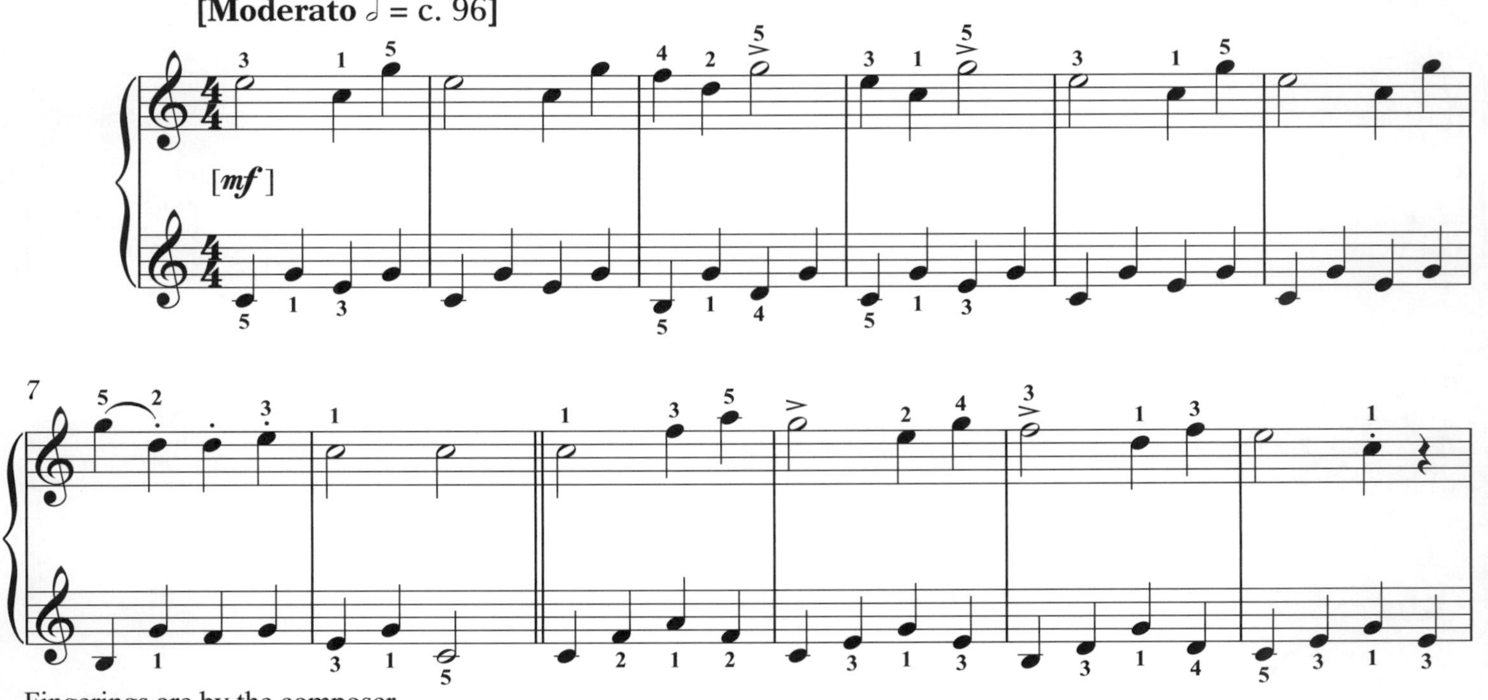

Fingerings are by the composer.

Exercise in C Major

from *The Little Pianist*

Carl Czerny
Op. 823, No. 6

[Larghetto 𝅗𝅥. = c. 60]

p

Fingerings are by the composer.

Lesson No. 3

from *The First Lessons*

Cornelius Gurlitt
Op. 117, No. 3

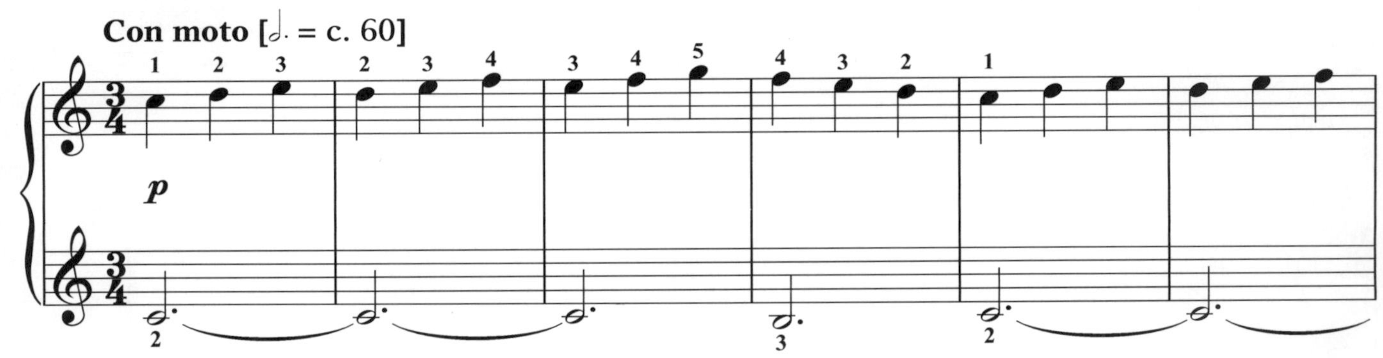

Fingerings are by the composer.

Lesson No. 9

from *The First Lessons*

Cornelius Gurlitt
Op. 117, No. 9

Fingerings are by the composer.

Follow the Leader

from *The First Term at the Piano*

Béla Bartók

[Adagietto] ♩ = 66

Fingerings are by the composer.

Invention I

from *The First Term at the Piano*

Béla Bartók

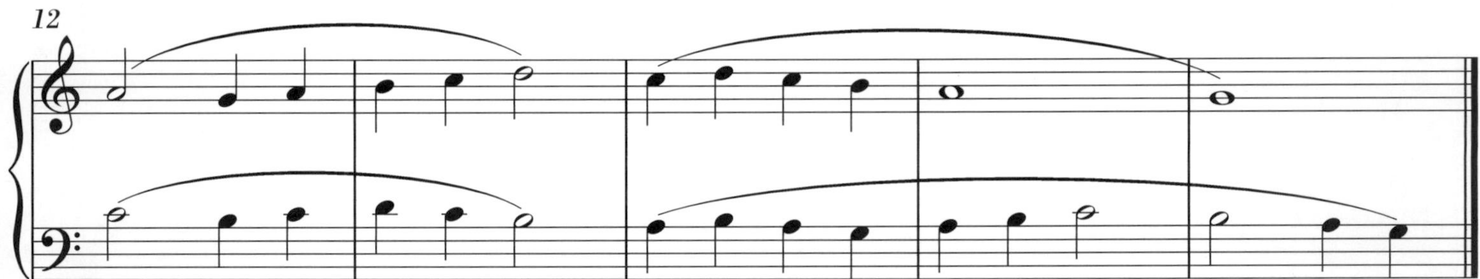

Fingerings are by the composer.

Passepied in C Major

George Frideric Handel
HWV 559

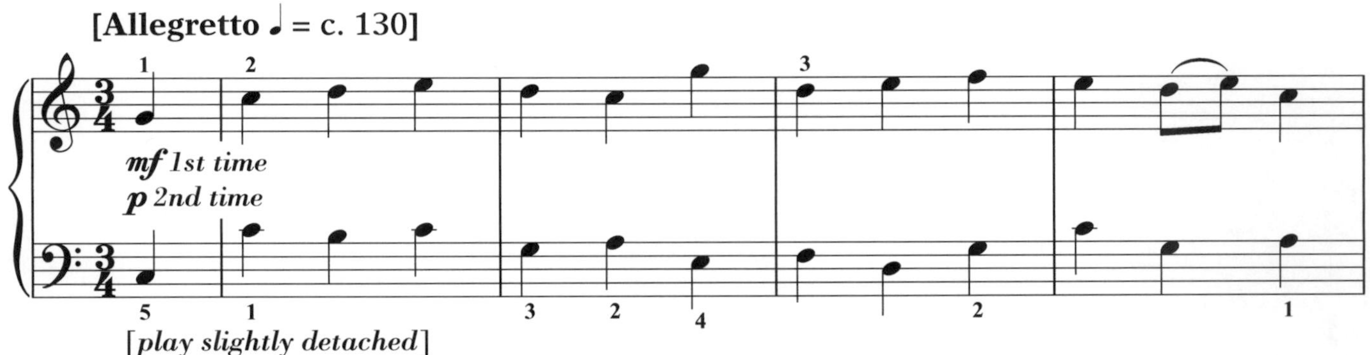

Articulations, dynamics, and fingerings are editorial suggestions.

The Scales

from *120 Pieces for the Aspiring Pianist*

Daniel Gottlob Türk
No. 6

Allegro non troppo [♩ = c. 120]

[*p*]

[*mf*]

Fingerings are by the composer. Dynamics and phrasing are editorial suggestions.

Lesson No. 6
from *The First Lessons*

Cornelius Gurlitt
Op. 117, No. 6

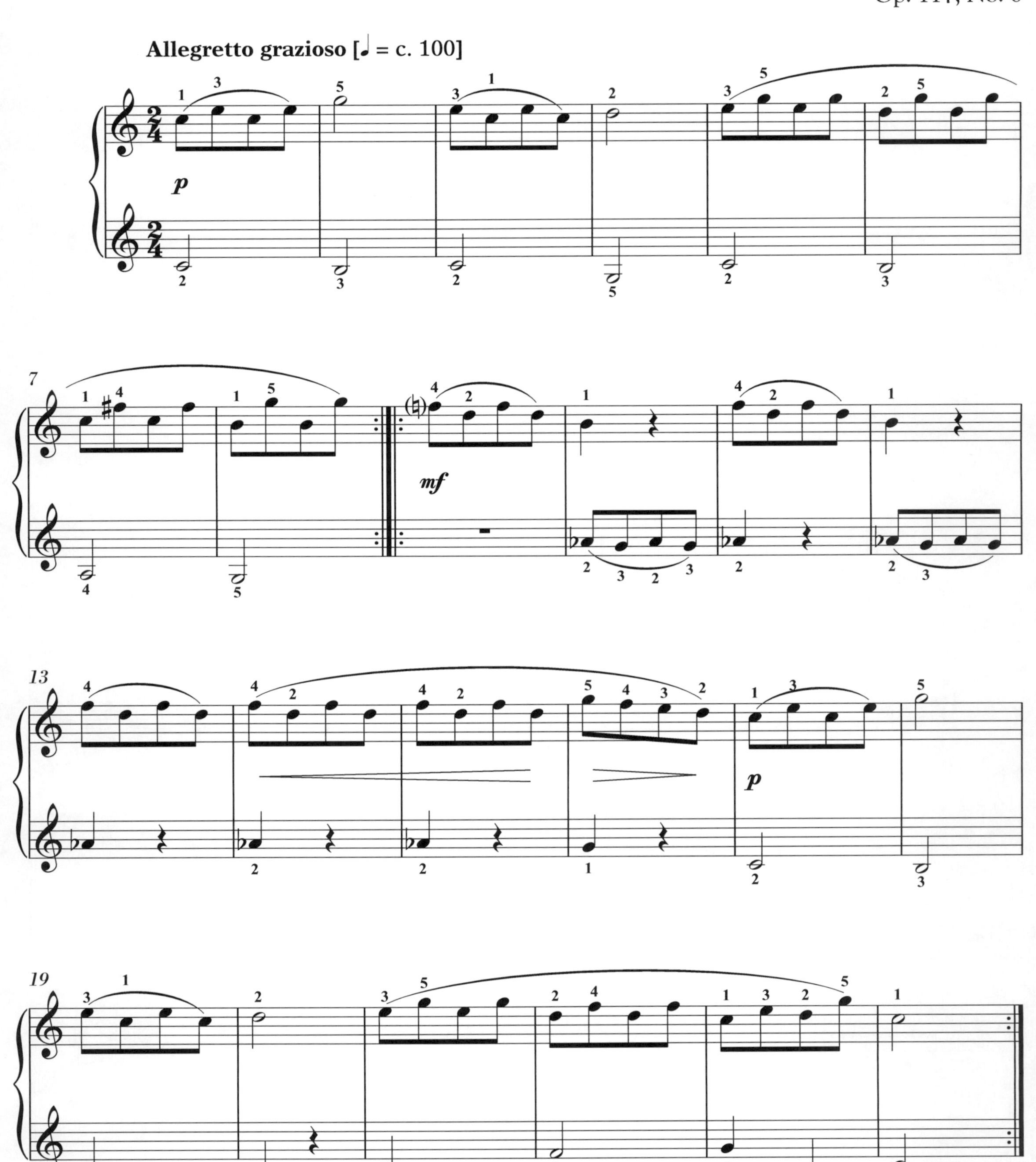

Fingerings are by the composer.

Imitation

from *The Easiest Exercises*

Louis Köhler
Op. 190, Nos. 13 and 14

Fingerings are by the composer. Dynamics and articulations are editorial suggestions.

Sad Feelings

from *120 Pieces for the Aspiring Pianist*

Daniel Gottlob Türk
No. 14

Poco Adagio [♩ = c. 56]

p [*legato*]

sfz *p* *sfz* *p*

Fingerings are by the composer.

Short and Long Legato
from *The First Term at the Piano*

Béla Bartók

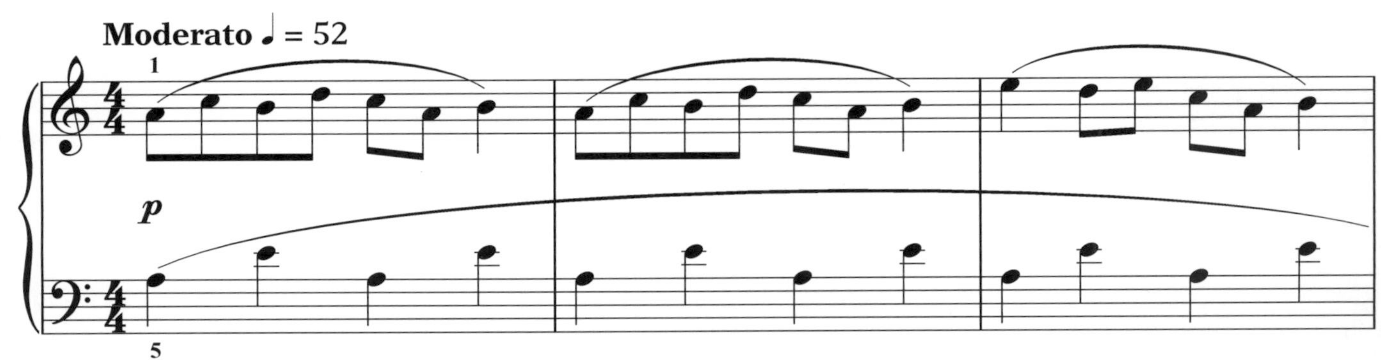

Fingerings are by the composer.

Trumpet and Drum
from *35 Easy Pieces*

Dmitri Kabalevsky
Op. 89, No. 20

Marziale [𝅗𝅥 = c. 72]

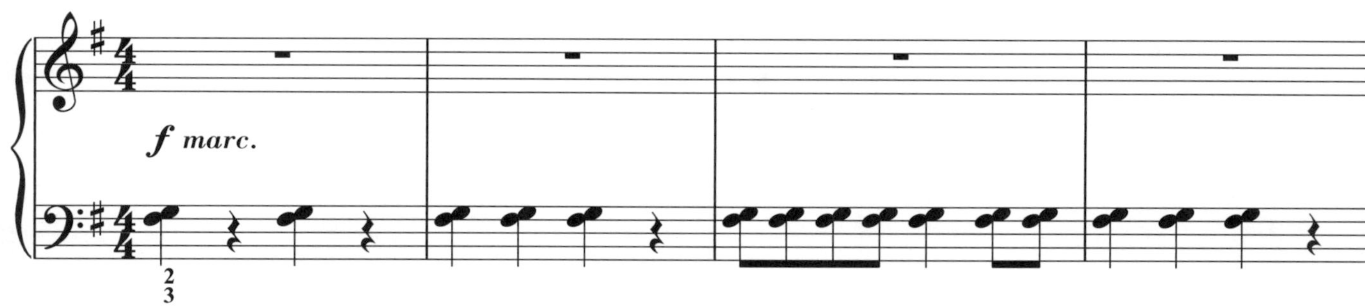

Fingerings are by the composer.

Scherzo

from *24 Pieces for Children*

Dmitri Kabalevsky
Op. 39, No. 12

Fingerings are editorial suggestions.

Waltz

from *Children's Notebook for Piano*

Dmitri Shostakovich
Op. 69, No. 2

Fingerings are by the composer.

Fanfare Rondeau

Jean-Joseph Mouret
arranged by Richard Walters

16
3
1 2 1
p

20
5
1 2 1
cresc.

24
4
f

28
poco rit.

March

from *Children's Notebook for Piano*

Dmitri Shostakovich
Op. 69, No. 1

Fingerings are by the composer.